WRIGHT MORRIS
Photographs & Words

BOOKS BY WRIGHT MORRIS

Novels

MY UNCLE DUDLEY, 1942
THE MAN WHO WAS THERE, 1945
THE WORLD IN THE ATTIC, 1949
MAN AND BOY, 1951
THE WORKS OF LOVE, 1952
THE DEEP SLEEP, 1953
THE HUGE SEASON, 1954
THE FIELD OF VISION, 1956
LOVE AMONG THE CANNIBALS, 1957
CEREMONY IN LONE TREE, 1960
WHAT A WAY TO GO, 1962
CAUSE FOR WONDER, 1963
ONE DAY, 1965
IN ORBIT, 1967
FIRE SERMON, 1971
WAR GAMES, 1972
A LIFE, 1973
THE FORK RIVER SPACE PROJECT, 1977
PLAINS SONG, 1980

Photo-Text

THE INHABITANTS, 1946
THE HOME PLACE, 1948
GOD'S COUNTRY AND MY PEOPLE, 1968
LOVE AFFAIR: A VENETIAN JOURNAL, 1972

Essays

THE TERRITORY AHEAD, 1958
A BILL OF RITES, A BILL OF WRONGS, A BILL OF GOODS, 1968
ABOUT FICTION, 1975
EARTHLY DELIGHTS, UNEARTHLY ADORNMENTS, 1978

Short Stories

REAL LOSSES, IMAGINARY GAINS, 1976

Memoirs

WILL'S BOY, 1981

Anthologies

WRIGHT MORRIS: A READER, 1970

WRIGHT MORRIS

Photographs & Words

Edited and with an Introduction by James Alinder

PUBLISHED BY THE FRIENDS OF PHOTOGRAPHY
IN ASSOCIATION WITH MATRIX PUBLICATIONS

ISBN 0-933286-28-7 (cloth); ISBN 0-933286-31-7 (paper)
Library of Congress Catalogue Card No. 82-082471

Design: Peter A. Andersen
Design Consultant: Eleanor Caponigro
Printing: Gardner/Fulmer Lithograph

This book is funded in part by a generous grant from the
National Endowment for the Arts, a federal agency.

Introduction

JAMES ALINDER

In the hands of Wright Morris, the recording qualities of the camera increase our willingness to accept the photograph as a mirror image, as an object of feeling and emotion. The organization of his images is classic; they are clear, precise and well constructed. Morris is drawn to the structures and artifacts of early decades, to used and worn objects that have been shaped by human experience and association or to abandoned buildings whose lives seem to have been played out. His role is to make the evidence clear and to communicate it directly. The photographs inform us, yet move us. They succeed not simply as visual documentation, but as works of art. While each makes a particular statement about the objects photographed, it also makes a general statement about the ceaseless replacement of objects in our culture.

A few of Morris' photographs resemble those identified with the Depression of the 1930s and the photographers of the Farm Security Administration. This is both understandable and misleading. The structures and artifacts may seem similar, but they are seen from a different perspective. In Morris the depressed social reality is subordinate to the revelation of experience. For him these images are life enhancing, rather than life depressing: expressive of great expectations as well as intractable human conditions.

Wright Morris was born on January 6, 1910, in Central City, Nebraska. At the age of nine he and his father moved from their rural home town to Omaha, and at fifteen they moved on to Chicago. In 1930 Morris left the Middle West to attend college in California. His roots in Nebraska were crucial to his development as a novelist, and provided the inspiration for many of his photographs.

Morris' growth as a photographer occurred at the same time as his development as a writer. While the recognition accorded his photographs has been substantial, his larger reputation rests on his preeminence as a novelist. He has written many books, and has twice received the coveted American Book Award—for *The Field of Vision* in 1956 and for *Plains Song* in 1981. His combination of text material with powerful pictures has made a unique contribution to the history of photography.

In 1938 Morris drove to the East Coast. The trip by car proved a revelation.

I saw the American landscape crowded with ruins I wanted to salvage. The depression created a world of objects toward which I felt affectionate and possessive. I ran a high fever of enthusiasm and believed myself chosen to record this history before it was gone.

Morris bought a 3¼ x 4¼ view camera with a wide angle lens, and his photographic document of America's structures and artifacts began with vigor. For some time he had been writing poetically dense prose paragraphs. He realized the direct relationship that existed between his writing and his photographs. In combination, the meaning of each was enhanced by the other, yet neither was used to directly explain the other. The visual and the written images could be joined in the mind's eye.

Work on this new idea developed into a photo-text project—the term is Morris'—called *The Inhabitants*. A Guggenheim Fellowship in photography was granted to Morris in 1942. The title and theme for the project was inspired by a passage from Thoreau's *Walden*.

What of architectural beauty I now see, I know has gradually grown from within outward, out of the necessities and character of the indweller, who is the only builder . . . it is the life of the inhabitants whose shells they are. . . .

Although Morris finished *The Inhabitants* in 1942, it was not published until after the war. In the meantime, his first two novels were released—*My Uncle Dudley* in 1942 and *The Man Who Was There* in 1945. Issued in 1946 by Scribner's, *The Inhabitants* was produced as a large format art book, printed on the best varnished oatmeal-colored paper available in the post-war era. It sold for $3.75.

In 1947 Morris received a second Guggenheim to extend the possibilities of the photo-text. For *The Home Place* Morris used a 4 x 5 view camera. Beginning in 1942, he photographed in and around the community of Chapman, Nebraska, and talked to local residents. He had many long conversations with the town barber, Eddie Cahow, who had known his mother and father. Through these experiences in small Nebraska towns his roots became concrete and communicable. "I had known little about my past except what I had conjured up in my fiction." The photographs from these sometimes extended visits documenting the fabric of rural American life are among Morris' most important work.

A significant number of the photographs from the project were made during a few intensely productive weeks in April and May of 1947 at the home place, his Uncle Harry's farm near Norfolk, and at the neighboring Ed's place. For such a quantity of great photographs to be made during such a short period represents an important achievement in the history of photography. Realizing the special and unique opportunity available around Chapman, Morris made the most of it. The experience and understanding he had accumulated during his previous decade were summarized, and to a great extent, finalized, in these images.

In the book *The Home Place* Morris used the smaller format of the novel rather than that of the larger picture book. The text is in the form of a narrative, and each page is faced by a photograph. The photo-text relationship is both explicit and evocative of life on a plains "dirt farm". *The Home Place* was published in 1948.

Almost all photographers important to the history of the medium have had an intense period of productivity of a relatively short duration. This is, in fact, the case with Wright Morris, who was for a decade, from 1938 to 1947, deeply involved in producing these remarkable photographs. There were some tentative works before that time, and a few parting gestures afterward, but it was during these years that the vast majority of his important photographs were made.

Morris continued to make photographs into the 1950s but as the demands of his career as a novelist increased, he pursued photography with less intensity. In 1954 he traveled to Mexico on a third Guggenheim. He had planned to photograph intensively there, but after a few exposures he became so involved in writing a novel that he put those plans aside.

Some two decades elapsed before Morris again combined words and pictures. Partly because of the constant demand for *The Inhabitants* and *The Home Place*, both of which had long been out-of-print, but also because he felt that time had put a different perspective on his writing, Morris created a new text to go with a selection of his earlier photographs. This third photo-text book, *God's Country and My People*, was published by Harper & Row in 1968. *God's Country* is the summation of Morris' photo-text statement. All three photo-text books are currently available in reprints.

In 1972 Morris published *Love Affair: A Venetian Journal*, a book of color photographs with a text concerned with the experiences he and his wife Jo had on the several occasions they lived in Venice.

For the past thirty years, writing has been Morris' first priority. During the 1960s and early 1970s, before his retirement in 1975, he taught creative writing at San Francisco State University. In recent years he has been sought out by a great number of university and other groups to speak on both writing and photography. While he strictly limits these occasions, his increasing popularity is based on his remarkable speaking abilities. Audiences are completely captivated by the depth of his ideas as well as by the flow of his language.

Morris' reputation as a writer lies in his ability to fabricate the rich texture of life; his unique intimacy with life on the plains is similarly demonstrated in his three photo-text volumes. The following excerpts from *God's Country and My People* exemplify this proficiency and are representative of Morris' historic contribution to literature.

There's little to see, but things leave an impression. It's a matter of time and repetition. As something old wears thin or out, something new wears in. The handle on the pump, the crank on the churn, the dipper floating in the bucket, the latch on the screen, the door on the privy, the fender on the stove, the knees of the pants and the seat of the chair, the handle of the brush and the lid to the pot exist in time but outside taste; they wear in more than they wear out. It can't be helped. It's neither good nor bad. It's the nature of life.

And,

A pattern for living, the blueprint of it, can be seen in the white stitches of the denim, the timepiece stamped like a medallion in the bib of the overalls. Between wearing something in and wearing it out the line is as vague as the receding horizon, and as hard to account for as the missing hairs of a brush.

In *Photographs and Words* the two principal preoccupations of Morris' career, sometimes complimentary, sometimes competitive, are found at ease in neutral corners. Each speaks for itself, the photographs with unexampled brilliance and fidelity, the words in a mood of affectionate reminiscence. For the reader and viewer it is a happy occasion. Morris writes for the first time, in some detail, of the complex ideas that have shaped his books of photographs and texts, and are equally manifest in his novels. The writer who began, as he tells us, to visualize the picture he would put into words, has always been the writer who has put into words what cries to be visualized. The selection of photographs reproduced in this volume presents with elegance, clarity and precision what the camera's eye, and the writer's eye, perceive in the visible world. If we see "images" more clearly than we do the world around us, as Morris has commented, it is thanks to the powers of the camera and such photographs as we find in this book.

Words

Photography in My Life

Wright Morris

In October of 1933 my room on Florianigasse in Vienna looked out on a small garden where the blind came to walk. When my bedding was aired at the casement in the morning I would lean out and observe them. They walked in pairs, stiffly erect, marching slowly to an unheard music. It shamed me to spy on them in this manner, but I was young, each hour seemed precious and I was eager to be one of those on whom nothing was lost. To hold fast to what might escape me, what I needed (I thought) was a camera.

A few weeks previously I had sailed from New York to Antwerp, spent a week in Paris, then came on to Vienna where I planned to spend the winter. A Viennese gentleman I had met on the freighter had assured me that I could live cheaply in Vienna, and he was right. I was still alive on $20 a month.

At twenty-three years of age and healthy I was prepared for hard and lean times, but my college years in California had reduced my tolerance for cold. My room was unheated. A tile oven, blue with chill, sat in the corner near the door, while I, propped up in bed, conjugated German verbs. My first unforeseen expense was for a flannel bathrobe, which I wore as a lining to my raincoat: my second unforeseen expense was a camera. I believe it was called a Zeiss Kolibri. What I highly admired was the styling, which bore little resemblance to a Kodak. On a grey chill day in an open air market, I found three peasant women, their heads wrapped in babushkas, standing behind the fat plucked geese they were selling. That picture—not quite in focus—is one I still have. Those taken from my window, of the *blindgarten*, have disappeared. Some four months later, in a prison in Grossetto, Italy, I would watch one of the prison officials open my camera and expose the film to the light, as he looked for "pictures". That took care of my effort not to lose the Leaning Tower of Pisa, or my friend astride his bicycle. I did manage to take some shots of the streets of Naples, and of the tree lined avenues of Paris, which I had enlarged to 5 x 7 inches and artfully printed on sepia paper. I was taking photographs of photographs I had previously seen. With one self-portrait taken in Capri, where I faced east across the Bay of Naples, once back in California I could reassure myself that I had actually been in Europe.

Some fifteen months later I applied the Zeiss Kolibri to the purchase of a Rolleiflex. I was a writer—what need did I have for a camera? For some four or five months I had been obsessed with a childhood, previously of no interest to me: my own. Page after page accumulated as I tried to recover my Nebraska boyhood. Most of these impressions were little more than sketches, verbal pictures of places, of time-stopped moments.

She wiped the table with the dish rag then leaned there, propped on her spread arms. A few leaves rattled in the yard. Some dirty leghorns clucked and waited at the screen. She left the rag on the table and emptied the pan toward the leaky shade. She stood there awhile, her hands pressed into the small of her back. Turning, she looked down the trail bright now with copper leaves at an old man's knees, white in the sun. She watched his brown hands lift Monkey Ward's, tear out a page. She watched him read both sides, very slowly, then tip his head. As he rose his overalls came up with a sigh and one strap hung swinging between his legs. She watched him step into the sun and hook it up. From his hat he took a feather and passed it through the stem of his pipe, then turned to strike the match on the door.

As I gathered these impressions it became apparent that I was making images with the characteristics of photographs, such as the eye for detail and the aura of detachment, of impersonal observation. It was clear to me, however, that a writer who wanted a *picture* of something might well *take* it rather than describe it. The pictures I wanted were back in the rural midwest, but I saw similar objects in the alleys and streets of Southern California. With the Rolleiflex camera, on a tripod, I began to search them out. Stoops and doorways, windows and screens, the tubs, tools and utensils of daily living, fences and gates, the patterns formed by light and shadow, verticals and horizontals. My assurance in this matter was puzzling. Except for the image on my mind's eye, I had no example or precedent. I had seen a few of Weston's photographs, but nothing by Dorothea Lange, Walker Evans or the photographers of the Farm Security Administration. Nor did it cross my mind to take pictures of people. I made enlargements of the prints that seemed more interesting than others, and from the deficiencies of what I had done I learned to see the limitations of what I was doing. One limitation was technical. I had yet to learn about the view camera and wide angle lenses. On occasional trips to Los Angeles I saw structures that excited me more than the familiar fragments, but I lacked the equipment to deal with such subjects. My first wife Mary Ellen and I were part of, but only moderately aware of, the Depression; she gave piano lessons, I worked part time for the WPA and continued working on a long novel. We thought we lived quite well on an income of sixty-five dollars a month.

In the summer of 1938 my wife accepted a position to teach at the Westover School in Middlebury, Connecticut. We went east by car, and had our first good look at the pueblo culture of the southwest. Along the way I took the picture of the fire hydrant and the barber pole in Needles, California (PLATE 33). Pueblo structures were popular at the time with both photographers and artists, and I ran a fever of excitement on seeing the ruins of Mesa Verde. Adobe walls and textures, patterns of light and shadow, the dominance of the past in all aspects of the present, the palpable sense of time as a presence, made me more fully aware of what I was seeking in the transient ruins of my own culture. I wanted evidence of man in the artifacts that revealed his passing. I was also instinctively drawn to forms that were traditional and impersonal. My need to take up a position *fronting* these forms, as if they were symbolic facts, I accepted without question. This is expressed in Thoreau's statement:

If you stand right fronting and face to face to a fact, you will see the sun glimmer on both its surfaces, as if it were a scimitar, and feel its sweet edge dividing you through the heart and marrow, and so you will happily conclude your mortal career. Be it life or death, we crave only reality. . . .

I am a later witness to this same need. Where these elements combine in a single photograph I take the greatest pleasure in the resulting image. There are numerous examples. Some structures impress me as icons, with a sense of their own—in the words of Henry James—a mystic meaning proper to themselves to give out. The meeting house in Southbury, Connecticut (PLATE 42); the Gano grain elevator in Kansas (PLATE 30); the house near McCook, Nebraska (PLATE 25); the rear of the Model T Ford (PLATE 22), the white house in Wellfleet (PLATE 44), are examples of this expressive form. Objects share this quality, singly or in groups, where exposure to human use has shaped them. The straight backed chair (PLATE 14), the drawer of silverware (PLATE 15), the bureau drawer at Ed's place (PLATE 11), Cahow's barber chair (PLATE 34). . . . The simplest snapshot will bear it witness, and we feel this directly, without mediation. In the Pueblo country I was able to sense more of my own inscrutable purpose. The worn and abandoned aroused me. Ten years before I returned to the home place, the farm near Norfolk, Nebraska, I was prepared to appreciate home-grown American ruins and to attempt to salvage what was vanishing. Nothing will compare with the photograph to register what is going, going, but not yet gone. The pathos of this moment, the reluctance of parting, we feel intensely.

After the years in Southern California the green landscape of New England seemed overwhelming. We spent the summer in Wellfleet, on the Cape, where I was seized with the desire to paint. Some of my California friends were painters, and predictably I attempted to paint what I would have photographed. Cape Cod houses and churches, the dunes of Truro, the white on chalk white, in a shimmer of sea air, would take a lifetime to fathom and another life to master. I was pleased with my bundle of amateur watercolors and stopped to show them to Lewis Mumford, who tactfully inquired about my photographs. I spent that winter in a cabin on Quassapaug Pond, working on a long novel, and the following summer, back in Wellfleet, I took pictures with my first 4 x 5 view camera. The bellows leaked, but I was able to see the beckoning promise on the ground glass.

In the fall, working on enlargements in a Middlebury farmhouse, I glimpsed the connection between words, my own written words, and the photographs I was taking. Rather than ponder the photograph, then describe my impressions, I found in what I had written the verbal images that enhanced, and enlarged upon, the photograph. The unexpected resonance and play between apparent contraries, and unrelated impressions, was precisely what delighted the imagination. I saw that this was often equally true of the pairings of friends, pets and lovers. In the unanticipated commingling of opposites the element of surprise was life enhancing.

I made a selection of the prints and mounted them with the related text attached. Learning that James Laughlin, of New Directions, was living nearby, I drove over with some examples to show him what I was doing. It did seem to be a new direction. After some reflection he agreed to publish a selection. The introduction I contributed has the tone of a Futurist manifesto, one of many that left the waiting world unchanged.

Laughlin's interest in my photo-text project, along with the results I was getting with my first Schneider-Angulon lens, led me to put my writing aside and to concentrate on *The Inhabitants*. I had in mind a volume of structures and artifacts that would represent the nation as a whole, having seen enough of them in my travels to know how diverse yet characteristic American structures would prove to be. Thoreau's comment is pertinent:

What of architectural beauty I now see, I know has gradually grown from within outward, out of the necessities and character of the indweller, who is the only builder— out of some unconscious truthfulness, and nobleness, without ever a thought for the appearance and whatever additional beauty of this kind is destined to be produced will be preceded by a like unconscious beauty of life . . . it is the life of the inhabitants whose shells they are. . . .

In the spring of 1939 I had brought a selection of *The Inhabitants* to New York, where I showed them to Beaumont Newhall at The Museum of Modern Art. Sometime later my wife and I visited Beaumont and Nancy Newhall and their handsome black cat Euripides Pants at their nearby apartment. I had met both Stieglitz and Dorothy Norman at An American Place, and at one of the soirees at her home on 71st Street, among a gathering of writers, painters and composers, I first met Ansel Adams. Almost forty years would pass before I saw him again, at his home in Carmel, California.

The Midwest and the Southwest, rural and urban, the marvelous houses and barns of New England I had just discovered, but I had seen little of the South except through photographs. Those of Walker Evans, in *American Photographs*, had profoundly confirmed my own responses. I did not see through Evans' eyes, but I was captive of the same materials. The Depression was spectacularly photogenic, and in *Life* magazine I had seen examples of the unmatched power of the camera eye. I also felt the urgency of the true believer about to voyage among the heathen. So many structures (souls) eager and willing to be saved might otherwise be lost! I had watched a barn collapse while I hastened to set up my camera. A strong whiff of missionary zeal fueled my enterprise. My ambitions were large but, fortunately, my means were small, or I might still be lost in the streets of Charleston or the back roads and trails of the Smokies.

In realistic terms, I planned a trip of some eight or ten thousand miles, beginning in the fall of 1940, going south to Georgia, west to Mississippi, north along the river to Nebraska, then southwest through Kansas, New Mexico and Arizona, to California, where I would spend the winter. In early spring I would head east, through Nevada, Utah, Idaho and Wyoming, crossing the plains while the trees were still barren, following the back roads through the farms of Iowa, Indiana and Illinois. I hoped to take as many as a thousand pictures selected from thousands of subjects. I wanted the representative structure that would speak for the numberless variations. I had in mind not one book, but a series, each dealing with a phase of our national life as I had experienced it. Rural, small town, urban and the open road. This first book, *The Inhabitants*, would be a survey of the state of the union in terms of its threatened symbols. How well I visualized it! There was no limit to my confidence, my enthusiasm, and combined with my sense of mission I was a formidable supplicant, able to persuade Louise Dillingham, the head of the Westover School, where my wife was teaching, to contribute $500 to this new direction of photographs and words. A '34 Ford coupe, with a rebuilt motor, the seat wide enough for me to curl up in, was fitted out with recapped tires and a South Wind heater. In October, with a carton of film packs, a 3¼ x 4¼ Graphic View, fitted with the Schneider Angulon lens, I stopped along Route 1, in New Jersey, to wait for a break in the flow of traffic to photograph the gleaming facade of a white church (PLATE 45). As so often before, another traveler was about to discover America.

In Washington, D.C., I stopped to see Roy Stryker, of the Farm Security Administration, who had provided employment for a unique assembly of photographers and directed them to an inexhaustible subject. I had fancied I might get a roving assignment from him, or at least wangle a supply of film. He looked at my examples with interest, but without enthusiasm. My conception of words and photographs puzzled him, and he was profoundly bemused by the absence of *people*. People, he said, were what it was all about. I agreed. Having seen thousands of exceptional photographs, those that I showed him did not overwhelm him. I tried to explain that the presence of people in the houses and barns was enhanced by their absence in the photographs. He had heard many things, but nothing so far-fetched as that. A profoundly compassionate man, increasingly aware of the sufferings of millions of Americans, he had little patience for what he felt to be suggestively "arty" in my photographs and texts. His programs hoped to correct social abuses, not serve as an excuse for personal experiment. He was not so blunt, but I understood his meaning. He was also correct in sensing that my purpose was not in the interests of social justice. I wanted the *persona* behind the social abuses, one that would prove to be the same with or without them. We were each right, in terms of what we wanted, and I left his office empty handed. One of Stryker's photographers, who had caught glimpses of my work, followed me out to the street and spoke to me. He said he liked what he had seen, and that I should not be discouraged. Regrettably, I have forgotten this man's name.

For reasons Stryker would not have approved, I took pictures of the box-like Civil War period houses in the Capitol's slums. I felt, thanks to Stryker, some embarrassment in the pleasure these shabby, dilapidated, lean-to dwellings gave me in the light of the social abuses they revealed. This dilemma, like so many, is part of our complex inscrutable human natures, and will not be resolved by legislation or discussion. The way I see what I photograph is to me life-enhancing. Other ways of seeing are equally valid, but they are not mine.

I spent that night parked at the end of a street, in suburban Alexandria, which proved to be a meeting place for spooners. Cars came and went during the night, their lights flashing on and off in my upward tilted rear view mirror. Of what did I think? Now and then I heard the music on their car radios.

With my interest in the old, the worn and worn out, the declined, the time-ravaged, the eroded and blighted, the used, abused and abandoned, as well as the structured volumes, the contrasts in texture, the endless gradations from black to white in stone, shingle, clapboard, painted or peeling, such as the rows of wooden and marble stoops in Baltimore (PLATE 57), after the first extended day of photographing my problem was more practical than esthetic. There seemed to be an inexhaustible bounty of material. I had a finite supply of film. I would have to be selective, wherever I looked, or my march through the South would end up like Sherman's, in Georgia.

The over-rich compost of Southern life and history, which I had sampled in the pages of Faulkner, was visible on the surface, in stratified layers, even for a traveler as ignorant as I. Southern atmosphere, as dense and pungent as leaf smoke, to be breathed in and savored like pollen, was in such contrast to my previous experience that I found myself in another country. The surface hospitality, the inflection of the language, the suspicion that there was less just below the surface than on the surface, the provocative sexuality that was a matter of custom, of tradition, not intended to incite more than a flirtation. The warm Southern nights, the music and the black voices seemed as exotic to me as I had found Mexico the previous summer.

Soon enough I discovered I was seen as an intruding alien. The camera, and the camera eye, is justly looked upon with suspicion. I tramped about with this machine, mounted on its tripod, and set it up to conceal myself beneath the hood, invariably pointed at some house or doorway judged to be of no pictorial interest. Why would I take *that*, except to reveal what was better concealed? I could only have in mind the exposure of whoever lived there, a blot on the peeling Southern escutcheon. As their attention turned from me to my car, with its out-of-state license, the picture seemed clear. I was a Northern snooper out to disfigure the troubled, dilapidated Southern self-image. Black and white both felt it, the black with less malice but a more profound discomfort. My presence testified to their worst suspicions about their own condition. The separate yet commingled cultures of black and white that make the South a unique and a tormented culture were at once unavoidably visible and subject to instant falsification. The impoverished black, the debased poor white, had been well exposed in books and magazines, and such distinctions as might be made were in the eye of the beholder, not the camera.

At the edge of Culpeper, in West Virginia, I found a house and dead tree, equally husk-like, both appearing to date from Lee's surrender, that seemed to speak directly to my troubled state of mind. Was it a portrait, or a caricature? Did it reveal a state of soul or a state of abuse? I could see now one, now the other, by merely blinking my eyes. But in the basking sunshine of a Blue Ridge October I felt the ripeness and warmth of survival more than I felt the chill of inhuman custom. The meaning this structure had to give out was a many layered, many voiced passage of history, too dense and complex to do more than acknowledge, but in this surviving husk it was more life-enhancing than life-defeating.

But that was not all. What I had made, when the shutter clicked, was a photograph. It would be weeks before I saw the negative, and many months would pass before I made a print of what I had seen on the ground glass. Would that image restore my original impressions, or would they be replaced by others? To what extent would this new image, cut off from its surroundings, constitute a new structure? How much of the "reality" had it captured? How much had it ignored? Whether or not it had been my intent, I would end up with something *other* than what was here. It would be a new likeness, a remarkable approximation, a ponderable resemblance, but not a copy. This new image would testify to the photographer's inscrutable presence. I was not appreciative of these distinctions at the time I took the picture, and believed that what I had seen on the ground glass would surely be what I had captured.

I was working on the faith and enthusiasm that what I saw on the ground glass would prove to be the photograph I wanted. Once a week, if possible, I would stop in a town where my film packs of negatives could be developed, and I could be reassured as to what I was doing. Ideally, I would have carried the developing equipment and periodically done the work myself. I had thought of that, and briefly tried it, but my interest in the chemistry side of photography was even less than my talent for it. I had neither the experience nor the confidence to do this crucial work myself. With few, and infrequent, exceptions, the method I had chosen proved to be the right one.

I made my way south along the foothills of the Smokies, the blues of the mountains to the west transparent in the hazy light, deepening to purple as the sun set behind them. The warmth of the season, the golden October light, the harmony that prevailed between man and nature (man and man was another matter) seemed to clarify for me, in an instant, the attachment of the Southerner to where he had come from. A ballad-like sense of peace, if not plenty, seemed as palpable to me as strains of music. I was subject, as my experience had proved, to a lyrical euphoria when exposed to such places. I had felt it repeatedly in Europe, and to the point of dazzlement in Mexico. If something unearthly had occurred, I would have been an eager and willing witness. This mood was both so tangible and so fragile I was reluctant to dispel it. I stayed away from the larger towns and avoided photographing what might arouse comment or suspicion. I confined myself to farmhouses and outbuildings, and to the look of fields and fences in the slanting light. I noted how frequently a coat of whitewash would accent a weathered wall, gate, door or brick chimney. Most of the natives I saw were black, deferential to whites and eager to be helpful. I soon found that their answers to my questions of where I was, and where I hoped to be going, were less concerned with information than with a desire to be cordial. Was this the right road? Yessuh. Was it a good road? Yessuh. If place names were mentioned I might not understand them and this increased my assurance of strangeness. I slept one night in the car—or rather I spent the night awake listening to the movement of cattle, the snuffling of curious dogs. My first night in a hotel, the bed a creaking antique on a floor that tilted toward the window, offered me a curtained view of the street that was like an illustration of a page of history. A white horse, ghostly in the light of a waning moon, whinnied in a manner I thought to be human. I relished the family style breakfast in the morning, which I shared with a guest and seven members of the family, having long forgotten what it was like to eat eggs fried in fat and hot slabs of cornbread. The affable garrulousness and easy hospitality charmed me. I liked being *huhhh-ney* to the woman who served me. I smoked a cigar that crackled like cornflakes when I lit it.

Two days later, on a Saturday night in North Carolina, I watched the town fill up with old cars, buggies and wagons that were full of denim-clad poor white country people and their children. It was new to me to see a real "tribe" of people, the men and women in separate groups, the kids roving about like unleashed pets, the men inclined to hunker down on their hams like Indians, their forearms on their knees, their hands dangling. It amazed me to see that they might crouch like that for an hour or more, silently smoking, or in animated talk. The women were never part of this commingling of the men. I liked the drawling speech, the turns of phrase and the breeding I saw in the lean faces and work-honed bodies, their postures and gestures acquired from the daily habits of a lifetime. I feared to intrude on them, but I liked spying on them as I would have gypsies in my home town. They seemed more interesting and intense than the people I had known. The women were lean from work and child rearing, the skin of their pale faces tight to the bones as if to emphasize fundamentals, thin-lipped, given to uneasy glances that might be quick to take offense. To watch them as intently as I cared to, I sat in the car pretending to read a paper. I wouldn't have dreamed of trying to take a picture. I had always felt the camera eye to be intrusive, but never so profoundly as when I contemplated directing it toward such private people. The barefooted children, in hand-me-down clothes, ran about beneath the wagons. How was it that I, a native of the plains, should feel that here I was, at long last, among my own people?

In South Carolina, near the state line, I stopped at the edge of a sun baked bean field. At its center, raised off the ground so high that a small child might walk beneath it, was a large, one-storied clapboard house with a shingled roof and high windows without glass. The windows made deep pockets of shade, and crisp shadows accented the unpainted clapboards. The yard around it was hard and swept clean as a floor, and between me and the house was a covered well with a pulley to raise and lower the galvanized bucket. Not a soul or a dog was in sight; in the high noonday heat I assumed both might be napping.

The patterns of light and shade, the colors of earth and wood, the shimmering flame of light at the edge of the shadows, compelled me to try and get the picture. In all of its weathered and man-shaped details it fulfilled my idea of the beautiful. But I would have to intrude on private property. Stealthily, picking my way along the furrows, extending the legs of the tripod as I approached the house, I set up my camera, stooped beneath the cloth and saw the blurred image on the ground glass. Beads of perspiration seeped into my eyes. I backed away, shirt-tailed my face, then once more focused on the ground glass. Just to the left of the house, perhaps ten yards behind it, in colors that appeared designed to conceal him, a black giant stood in a posture of resting, his hands clasping a hoe handle. A narrow brimmed hat, tilted forward, shaded his eyes. I pretended not to see him. It made my movements more assured and casual. I was deliberate and open in what I was doing. I moved the tripod, I took several pictures. I felt the passing of time would prove to be to my advantage. On the ground glass I watched him approach me until beads of perspiration burned my eyes. Too late to cut and run, I was paralyzed.

"What you see?" he asked me.

Out from under the cloth I peered up, and up, at the ivory smile in his black face. He was curious. "What you see?" he repeated.

"You want to look?" He did. He crouched low, I hooded him with the cloth, and for a long moment he was silent. Backing away, he shook his head, puzzled. "You don't see it?" He did not. I checked to see if the glass was in focus. It was beautiful. Then it occurred to me it was upside down. "It's upside down," I said, apologetic. That was more mystifying. He had another look at it. What he saw led him to stoop, slapping his knees, then straighten up with a bellow of laughter. Why the image was upside down was something I did not want to go into. We moved to the shady side of his well where we both had a drink from the bucket. He took deep audible swallows, his adam's apple pumping. When he had finished he emptied the bucket over his head, the spill of water darkening his shirt. The drops that fell to the ground did not soak in, but rolled into balls of dust. If he had worn a sheet I would have felt in the presence of the Lord in *Green Pastures*. Near where we stood, a wire supported pole I had not noticed went up about twenty feet to dangle four or five gourds, the narrow ends chopped off. Small birds, nesting in the gourds, darted in and out. He watched this with such delight and concentration I walked away, not wanting to disturb him, and when I looked back from the road he was still there, his wet hair gleaming.

A few hours later, in Greenville, I had my dinner in a cafe then walked around the streets as the day cooled. There were structures on the main street I planned to photograph in the morning, when the light would be better. The Southern night was breezeless and humid. It seemed foolish to spend it cooped up in a hotel room. I followed a dusty side road to the edge of town and parked just off the road, in the shade of a willow. Later I curled up in the seat and lay there attentive to the sounds that came from the nearby houses, the voices of children, dogs, radio programs. I had half drowsed off when lights flickered in the rear view mirror and the windshield. I heard the throb of an idle motor. A moment later a cop with a beefy, perspiring face put his head in the window I had opened. He noted my camera, set up at the ready, and the boots I had unlaced to cool my feet. Something about that pleased him. He turned to wag a finger at the cop he had left in the car.

"Hi," I said, and smiled.

In 1940 the second world war had begun, but we were not yet in it. A slight war fever was palpable among those who might be drafted or felt themselves threatened. In Greenville, South Carolina, I was picked up as a vagrant and charged with being a possible spy. My camera was there beside me and I had obviously been taking pictures. Of what? Of critical installations, surely. The excitement of having captured a spy soon gave rise to a sense of exhilaration. The chief of police, a short, fat man with a nervous hysterical manner, leather straps, ammunition belts, pistol in a holster, might have served Mack Sennett as a model for the comical, as opposed to the beefy and brutal, Southern cop.

I was finger-printed and questioned, and all of my gear was inventoried. Then I was taken to the second floor of a jail behind the buildings facing the main street. This was a single large room, with bars at the windows, cots placed around the walls, with a windowless cell, the door heavily barred, in the room's back corner. A local desperado, by the name of Furman, was kept in this cell.

In the room below, as I found out at sunrise, a chain gang of blacks was incarcerated. The racket they made leaving their quarters woke me up. We had a view through the door and the glassless windows over the lower roofs of the town. We could see and hear it come alive in the morning, pause during the heat of the day, become active and noisy approaching the dinner hour, then quiet down in the evening. I shared the room with a motley crew of bums, ne'er do wells and poor whites. They had been drinking and fighting, or merely loafing. Some were loud and bitter for as long as ten minutes. Most were resigned. During part of the day and the long night they were full of talk, tall tales and wild humor. Having me as a new and interested listener meant more than having me as a talker. I did a lot of listening and scratching. Once or twice a day I gave somber speeches to the chief of police as he stood at the door. He liked my performance. While I talked he chewed on a toothpick, dipped one hand to his crotch and gazed reflectively over the roofs of the city, surveying his domain.

On the strength of hoping I was a spy, a plainclothes official, a kindly elderly man with whom I briefly discussed Stark Young and Faulkner, came over from the capitol, Columbia. He looked at my papers, heard my story and recommended that I spend at least a week in Charleston, then advised them to release me. I had a long day and night to brood if that advice would ever be taken. On the third or fourth morning, shortly after the chain gang rattled its way down the alley, I had a tin cup of coffee with the chief. He had for me, he said, no hard feelings. He gave me my camera and the keys to my car, and advised me to get the hell out of South Carolina. That advice I took. Along with me went a large colony of bugs, some who took up fairly permanent residence. I drove without stopping, but with the greatest of care, the eighty miles or so to the Georgia state line, then another fifty miles or so to Athens. In the Athens YMCA I took a long, long shower and washed myself repeatedly with Lifebuoy soap, scrubbing my scalp and hair. The profound relief I felt—to be free of incarceration, of a sense of helplessness that is traumatic—had little or nothing to do with the relatively comical incident. I had known it earlier, in Grossetto, Italy, where I was picked up as a threat to Mussolini; but the jail in Greenville, the character of the law and order, the "outside" world that I could see and share through the windows, left on me a ponderable impression. Two months later, in Santa Fe, I put it into fiction. A year later it would become the closing chapter of a novel, *My Uncle Dudley*.

I was understandably reluctant to take pictures while in Georgia. I had heard about Georgia, I had read *Tobacco Road*, I had seen the chain gangs in the movies. I kept a low profile. I had recently read *The Heart is a Lonely Hunter* and heard that Carson McCullers had lived in Columbus. I could believe that. The basking Southern heat, the soft golden light, the way structures and people appeared to be saturated with the scent of a past as dense as leaf smoke, smoldering and drug-like, in which everybody was a willing compliant victim. Walking the dusty streets I envied the writers fortunate enough to come from such places, still sticky with the pollen that clung to them. It seemed to me they need only close their eyes, open their pores and inhale deeply to possess their subjects. The sorghum-like richness of Southern life was both on the surface and fermenting beneath it. Through the dusty lace curtains at my hotel room window I spied on passersby I secretly envied, as Sherwood Anderson spied on his neighbors in Winesberg. They were dream-drugged, these people, and I envied the depth of their addiction.

In the nearby countryside, as I was driving around, I saw the glow of lights that I thought might be a fire. It proved to be a small carnival, with a rocking, clanking ferris wheel, one or two dangerous rides and sideshows of freaks. It had been set up in a field of trampled grass, the air smoking with the savor of barbecued meat. No carnival or Chautauqua of my boyhood generated so much excitement and expectation. These countryfolk, with their throngs of small fry, were the crackers I had read about in Erskine Caldwell. I was amazed at the visible kinship linking the cartoon grotesqueries of Li'l Abner or the figures in Faulkner's *Spotted Horses* to the people I saw around me. In the context small occasions provided, larger than life figures and sentiments materialized. Given a throng of expectant, deprived rural people, a mythic South might emerge from their shared expectations. Its sensuality aroused me. I felt the surrounding darkness would soon be cluttered with amorous couples. After the engines had coughed and died, the crowd had dispersed and the tents had collapsed, a cloud of dust so thick I could taste it hung over the field where it had all happened. I spent the night in the car not far from a banjo that repeated, and repeated, the same chords. Now and then the player cried out in the manner of a flamenco singer. I largely owed to these few weeks of Southern exposure my feeling that hardship, and hard times, if not destructively brutal or prolonged to the point of negation, are necessary to a density and richness of emotion that seems noticeably absent in happier situations. I did not say to myself that my life had changed, but with the morning light I felt that it had. Missing from my life had been the emotion that finds its fulfillment and release in the ballad. I had discovered the emotion, but how to cultivate it would prove to be the work of a lifetime. A few years later when I had read James Agee's *Let Us Now Praise Famous Men* and had seen Walker Evans' accompanying photographs of the sharecroppers I would fully appreciate the wide range of impressions I had just experienced.

In Pike County, Alabama, I crossed a field of corn stubble to get a clear view of several barns and a house, weathered to the color of dead branches. I moved in closer to get the shingled roof of the house, shimmering with heat. Under the hood of the camera, focusing on the ground glass, I heard an angry, bellowing voice. I uncovered my head and looked around. I saw no one. The voice spoke again—it seemed closer—and the corn stubble crackled as if trampled by cattle. The blast that followed was that of a shotgun behind the barns. In the morning stillness the air seemed to tremble, and so did my legs and hands. I ran for the car, the tripod legs dragging, and some moments later I saw, with the wide, staring eyes, the film of perspiration on my face in the rear view mirror. Could one smell of fear? I thought I could detect it.

A Southern friend had told me that the streets of Montgomery were as fragrant with sex as with the smell of magnolia, and I drove about slowly, sniffing the air like a coon dog. The basking, windless heat was stirred only by fans, wagging in the shadows of deep porches. I drank a cold Dr. Pepper at a drugstore counter, the mirror vibrating with the throb of a ceiling fan, but I took no pictures. The postcard I had written and put a stamp on I decided not to mail.

My objective was New Orleans, and I persuaded myself that I should get there a day or so early. I drove south to Mobile, then west along the Gulf Coast, the water as smooth as a pond. Men and boys sat along the shore, fishing, with the lines dangling slack from their long poles. I had not experienced heat that drugged the senses and had about it a lulling, agreeable torpor. To keep from dozing at the wheel I parked and took a nap. Animals and people were both becalmed. I understood the necessity of the siesta. Much later I would understand the need for the bourbon and the mint julep.

In New Orleans I had been invited to stay with Otis Lee, who had been one of my teachers at Pomona College. That winter he was on leave from his position at Vassar to continue his own philosophical writing. The week I spent in New Orleans owed more to Otis and Dorothy Lee, and our long nightly discussions, than to the prowling with the camera in the *vieux carre*. I soaked up atmosphere to the point of saturation, but for reasons that are no longer clear to me I overexposed most of the negatives. The structures are still embedded in the film, waiting on a more patient darkroom attendant than I was at the time.

In November, driving north from New Orleans, I stopped to see a friend who was then living in Jackson, Mississippi. He took me to meet one of his friends and neighbors, Eudora Welty, and among other things we talked about William Faulkner. Faulkner's town was Oxford, on my route north, but I had no intention of intruding on his privacy. I was encouraged, however, to intrude, if possible, on his old friend Phil Stone. That also seemed unwarranted to me, as a writer who had as of then published nothing, so I spent most of the day in Oxford sitting in the square waiting for history to strike me. It did not. Late in the afternoon I screwed up enough gall, mixed with courage, to appear at the door of Stone's law office. He was there. On admitting my interest in Faulkner, I was taken in tow. Phil Stone was a fluent and accomplished talker, and like most talkers he craved a fresh and good listener, which I proved to be. I was directed to the house down the street, centered in a large lot, which now looms in my mind like a Faulknerian mansion, but unfortunately the details are blurred, and I took no pictures. My car was parked in the driveway approaching the house, where I assumed I would be spending the night. I would meet his wife. I would be modestly feted. I would be gorged with tales beyond the telling, and I would be dimly aware, during the long evening, of the ghostly passage of black figures and the musical murmur of black voices. Some time after midnight, not asked to stay, I inquired if I might spend the night in my car while it was parked in their drive. I had told them of my adventure in Greenville, South Carolina. I was given permission to sleep in my car.

I lay awake until daylight seeking a clue to my pleasurable but disordered impressions. In the light of these impressions, Faulkner's fiction seemed both controlled and understated. The soul of the South, as I was privileged to perceive it, seemed to me more complex, and bizarre, than the reports I had read about it. More incredible to me, I found its strangeness wondrous and life-enhancing, rather than merely monstrous and grotesque. I owed these impressions to Phil Stone's remarkable relationship with black people—*his* Negroes, who deliberately chose not to be free. A few were servants in his house, others occupied barns and outbuildings. Something in Phil Stone's nature cultivated and responded to this reversal of historical roles, the master who became the captive of his slaves. I had been greatly impressed by Melville's profound grasp of this dilemma in his novella, *Benito Cereno*, which I saw worked out with even greater refinement in the way the blacks dominated the Stone household. A marvelous "mammy", deep and broad as a scow, served the food she had prepared on a schedule of her own making, her eyes rolling, her lips parted in a litany of *yessuhs* and *yesmaams*. With each serving I exchanged knowing glances with the master and the mistress of the house, eager to share their predicament. An old black man named Blue, asked to fetch wood for a fire, appeared in an hour's time with a stick, no more than a piece of kindling, on his crossed arms like an offering. Thanked for that, but urged to get more, he almost collapsed with contrition, then appeared, an hour later, with two pieces of the same size.

I had been eagerly brought to the Stone house to share its hospitality, so that I could bear witness to this drama of the slaves who were now the masters, and seemed even more fawning in their service. The role reversal had been so complete, so lovingly achieved, that Stone felt compelled to share it with someone, even a profoundly ignorant youthful Yankee. He had become captivated by his own captivity. I doubt that this was true of his young wife, preoccupied with a squalling infant, but Stone took me off to his study for further comments on his condition. He was a friend of FDR and other national figures; their signed photographs ornamented the book lined room. We smoked stogies imported from Pennsylvania while he brought me up to date on his pleasurable torments. They were many. Periodically he sent the young black men to Memphis, with stakes of money, but once separated from the money they returned to his house. The external world did not appeal to them. Besides, they loved the master and the mistress. The top exhibit—for which I was slowly prepared—was a satin lined case full of silver goblets, each goblet twisted on its stem by powerful hands. Who had done it? The loving Mammy. It just seemed to happen and she couldn't help it. She was just giving each one of them a polish, and lo and behold it just seemed to happen. Two dozen goblets. It was clear to both of us that Mammy's twist had made them priceless.

Shortly after midnight his wife appeared to call him to bed. He bid me goodnight, wished me luck as a writer, and showed me to the door. Before I passed through it I managed to ask him again if I could sleep in my car, while it was parked in his driveway. Yes, that I could do. More than that, if I delayed my departure I might have breakfast with them in the morning. As I made myself comfortable in the seat of the car I wondered if this, too, was a decision that the slaves had made for the masters. A sleeping guest was a bother. There would be a bed to make, and sheets to be changed. By morning it was drizzling, and just after daylight I opened my eyes to see the aging, half-blind Blue at my window, peering in, muttering to himself. Did he see me? I pretended to sleep. When he shuffled off, in a parody of the gait of Stepin Fetchit, I decided to take off rather than weaken or dispel the incredible events of the evening. I had breakfast in Oxford, grits with my eggs, then drove north to where a bank near the road had eroded to leave a raw gully, red as a bleeding wound in the drizzle (PLATE 48). I badly wanted this image for *The Inhabitants*, and even as I worked to get the photograph I began to ponder a suitable text.

Perhaps an hour later, raining much harder, I passed a field where a harness-patched plow horse, white as Moby Dick, stood luminous in a piece of over-grazed pasture, his heavy head bowed. I should have stopped to photograph it. That I did not is why I have forever borne it so vividly in mind.

In Arkansas the rain-washed air dried as quickly as a water color. I took pictures of barns, mostly hog farms, the pens black and muddy, the hogs happy, the smell of the ripe manure as rich and juicy as chewed tobacco. I drove a long day, feeling the need of a change. Late at night, near the Missouri line, I parked off the road to sleep. At sunrise I awoke on the rim of the world. The shadow of the car stretched out before me, the light spreading like surf, splashing on objects. It may have been the first time I saw the plains as a metaphor for the sea, a place to be possessed by the imagination. I no more than saw it, I did not feel inspired by the sight to possess it, but coming out of the woods, literally and figuratively, where I had been wandering for more than six weeks, I experienced the prodigal son's elation at the sight of the homeland. I think it amused me. My view of the plains had always been dim. My sentiments on the occasional cross country drives were expressed in my early fiction, where Nebraska was the place one drove all night while your companion slept in the seat. That had been the impression of my friends in the east.

As the sun rose I found much to photograph, anything that stood up so the light would strike it—an almost audible clamor at sunrise—houses and barns, fences and telephone poles, clusters of trees and dwellings, and like a sail at sea, the occasional gleam of a grain elevator. I saw, but did not fully sense, that these constructions were pathetically temporary on the vast exposed landscape. In this I found their appeal, their life-enhancing poignancy. My instinct was to celebrate the eloquence of structures so plainly dedicated to human use, and to salvage those that were on the edge of dissolution. The plains provided a scenic prop that was free of obstruction, where the sun was sufficient to delineate the object. I took my subjects on the run, as the light fell on them, frequently not at all to their advantage, since I was eager to see what beckoned down the road and was apprehensive about a change in the weather. A rural schoolhouse, near Goodland, Kansas (PLATE 47), with its crisp volumes of white contrasted with deep shadows, spoke to me in the same classical terms as the white house in Wellfleet, on the Cape. No need for poignancy here, only visual delight, a clear statement of protestant principle and practice.

The roll and dip of the plains increased as I drove west, reminding me that my boyhood in the flat Platte Valley of Nebraska had given me a mistaken notion of the high plains. They were remarkably sealike, the towns sunbaked and windblown riding the crests of the waves. Near the Colorado border—it might have been Goodland—I found a row of stores (PLATE 32), with curtained and blind-drawn windows and slightly tilting false fronts, that would provide me with an inexhaustible image of plains character and experience, mute, implacable and yet expectant. Stubbornly and irrationally optimistic.

On the crests of the rise, as I drove south, I caught glimpses of an arrow that pointed at the sky, like a rocket on its pad, the moon its destination. As I moved closer I saw the staggered tiers of a grain elevator approximately in scale with the landscape. The freight train at its base was hardly visible. Only when I saw it enlarged and printed would I have a sense of its proportions (PLATE 30). An almost high noon light, filtered through an overcast, revealed the ripple in the sheet metal attached to the structure's surface. This enhanced the reflected shimmer of light. Near the top, appropriately enigmatic, the four letter word G A N O.

From the edge of the highway, several hundred yards away, I studied the image on the ground glass and took several pictures. My appreciation of what I judge a great image reveals itself in my concern that I might flaw the negative in the taking or in its development. Fortunately, this negative was not flawed, and the print is one I find gratifying. It speaks to me like an icon of the tensions that are overwhelmed by the scale of the landscape and seek release in flight. It can also just be looked at. The photograph, that is, since I am sure the structure itself is long gone. Grain is now stored in huge concrete silos that give a space-age accent to the surrounding plain, and frequently blow up.

Going over Raton Pass, south of Trinidad, Colorado, I recovered the excitement I had felt as a youth on my first car trip to California in the winter of 1926. From the mountains I could see the great blue and rose mesas, like camouflaged ships anchored on the high cloud-dappled New Mexico plateau. The emotions I felt would reassert themselves when I arrived in Los Angeles and found myself nostalgically pondering my early days and wonderful times on the open road.

In the winter of 1940 Santa Fe was still the town of old adobe houses, hot sun, cool shadows, a bandstand in the square, blankets and silver in the shops and Pueblo Indians crouched under the awning of the Governor's building. Most of the artists and writers had moved on to greener pastures or trickled back to Greenwich Village, but the lobby of the La Fonda Hotel thronged with trend-seeking tourists and self-proclaimed old timers. I listened to their stories. Mabel Dodge Luhan was at home near Taos, where the natives were reduced to Sears & Roebuck blankets. The air was like wine, the light shimmered like tinsel, and I marveled how I had dreamed of living anywhere else.

I found a room a ten minute walk from the square for $5 a week. The detail is part of the period's aura. I spent the sun-struck days visiting the pueblos, San Ildefonso, Santo Domingo, etc., or following dirt roads wherever they led me. Gas was cheap. My problem was conserving film. I watched Maria Martinez shape and fire her pottery, and bargained with Fred Kabotie for one of his paintings. In the evening I looked for a seat in the La Fonda lobby, fragrant with piñon fires and the smell of Mexican food. I loved the slap and creak of new and old huaraches. I had been in Oaxaca and Mexico City and felt myself one of the chosen.

The big event of the season was the world premiere of Errol Flynn and Olivia de Havilland in *The Oregon Trail*. This trail did not come to Santa Fe, but Hollywood did. The ceremony took place in the floodlit square white with the first snow, and ringed with Christmas lights. The Indian men and their women viewed the white man's fiesta with their customary resignation. Carols were played. Errol Flynn brushed against me as he made his way into the La Fonda lobby.

In a few weeks I had shot more film than I should have, and suffered from a bad case of pueblo country enchantment. I had bought some old pottery, some new blankets, and before the fever maimed me, or abated, I managed to take off. I drove through a starry night to Needles, California, where I had a fine breakfast in the Harvey House in the railroad station, one of the first and last sanctuaries of great coffee. As I drove west out of Needles I felt the resurgence of the old attraction. California, before I set eyes on it, had been for me the sanctuary of my great expectations, and my years at Pomona College had fired the clay of these impressions. Once I had crossed the mountains, and from Cajon Pass saw the haze of smudge pots over the valley, through which the tan eucalyptus trees thrust up like feathers, I was hooked. Old Baldy gleamed with a snow cap, and the trees were freighted with oranges and lemons. I stopped to drink my fill of orange juice for 15¢ and ask the price of avocados. They were a dime. In Claremont I drove slowly around the streets and thought the students attractive but extremely youthful. How long had it been since I had been one of them? Not quite five years. In the post office, with its WPA murals painted by Milford Zornes, a classmate, an old friend was so startled to see me I let myself pass for an imposter. In the mail I had received the New Directions volume with the selection of my photographs and texts, along with a brief review from The New Yorker in which my name was mentioned. A first on all counts. At the Sugar Bowl cafe I was recognized, and experienced the sensation of being interviewed. Fame, surely. I was treated to a piece of pecan pie. To prolong this occasion I sought out Hal Davis, one of my English teachers, who was very kindly and favorably impressed. In that far time publication was a singular event. Many were called, but few were chosen. I stayed with Hal for two days, smoking his cigarettes and giving him the lowdown on South Carolina hoosegows. The sight of my words in print had stirred banked fires and started other juices flowing. I was eager to write. What? The writing would flow out of my aroused nostalgia, the boy who had arrived, fifteen years before, with his father in the sidecar of a motorcycle.

In Los Angeles I found a light housekeeping room near Echo Lake Park. I put aside what I had begun in Santa Fe, an effort to recapture my days and nights in Greenville, and started a book that began:

When it was cold we walked around. When it was morning the pigeons came and looked but when nothing happened they walked away. When it was warm we sat in the sun.

That was the way it had been in 1926, and the passage of time had given it vintage. Would it prove to have the bouquet—on the green side—of my own wine? In two months I would write what would prove to be the first 150 pages of *My Uncle Dudley*, stopping where the car collapsed in Arkansas the morning the Mississippi broke through the levee. With a stint of writing done, I was both free and eager to turn back to photography. I should have waited several weeks, until a touch of spring had softened the weather east of the rockies, but I was anxious to rejoin my wife, who would meet me in Cleveland at the home of her parents, then set up a darkroom in New York and make my first prints from the negatives of the previous months' work.

I headed east in early March, driving northwest from Las Vegas through the mining and ghost towns to Virginia City. Overcast skies, strong winds and freezing cold discouraged much picture taking. I put up in the Comstock Lode Hotel in Virginia City, until a half day of brilliant sunlight gave me the half dozen pictures I was determined to get. One was the pair of weathered houses on an incline (PLATE 54), preserved in every detail like the mummies in Guanajuato. The other the abandoned church and Hudson-bracketed house stark against a landscape of desert and sky (PLATE 55), more in the style of the baroque than American gothic. With these trophies hopefully in the bag I headed northwest for Boise, Idaho, to visit my Aunt Winona, one of my mother's Seventh Day Adventist sisters. A single day with her, and other members of the clan, helped to restore the ties I had with my Nebraska boyhood. Near Pocatello, in a gale-like wind that twice toppled my camera, I managed to get a picture of a cattle shelter in a barren, forbidding landscape. Had the settler found water? There was nothing, anywhere, on which the eye could rest or the body find refuge. In such places I felt the settler's implacable commitment, like a symptom of madness, to self-destruction. He took on the elements. Anything less would not have gratified his consuming rage.

Blowing snow plagued me across Wyoming, piling up like confetti on the windshield wiper, and I lay awake on the whistling nights fueled by the day's eight or ten cups of coffee. Nebraska too was snow covered, but thawing, and I stopped frequently along the route to photograph houses lapped by waves of dirty snow. The planes and patterns of dormers and gables, in wraps of dirty ermine, were like winter portraits. Just east of Lincoln, on a rise north of the highway, I crossed a field of stubble to take the farmhouse against the blowing winter sky (PLATE 29). The roof tilted the snow in such a manner that it reflected a more intense light than the field. The warmth inside the house had helped to thaw a black rim around the roof snow that set it off like a frame, but I would not see these details clearly until they emerged in the darkroom, five or six weeks later.

Through friends I had discovered Brooklyn Heights on the East River. The brownstone houses on Columbia Street had apartments at the rear that overlooked the river and the Brooklyn Bridge. It seemed to me few landscapes were comparable. Hart Crane had lived on this street with other writers and poets, and I found a ground floor apartment that had just been repainted, at 196 Columbia Heights. In a few days it had been furnished with a set of springs, boxes for books, and some cushions. Chairs would wait on success. The first order of business was to set up a darkroom. I made the first 8 x 10 prints of the new negatives, using amidol as developer and Velour Black for my paper. I thought they looked pretty great.

I worked a long day, stopping in the late afternoon to walk across the Brooklyn Bridge to City Hall square, where I could find great bargains in panatella cigars. I lolled at my ease, Whitman style, savoring the smell of the leaf and the passing throng. I had learned about cigars the previous summer in Mexico and smoked them in the manner of Thomas Mann's Hans Castorp, appreciating the aroma of the leaf wrapper and the way the veins remained visible in the long white ash. I can't imagine how a well primed dreamer, feeling his oats, could have had it better. I felt very much in tune with my obsessions and assured about what I was doing. Edward Weston had recently won a Guggenheim Fellowship in photography, the first, and it had occurred to me that I might do the same. Such confidence is born of ignorance. I knew virtually nothing about photography but what I saw in the magazines. I was fortunate to have enough technique to make good prints from excellent negatives, and to know what I considered a photograph of interest. As the prints accumulated I expanded my collection of *Inhabitants* and worked on new texts. I wanted the volume to suggest the range and variety of the country. I was also rewriting the draft of the novel I had begun in Los Angeles. I liked its tonal consistency and the range of characters, but was it a long story or a novel? It seemed to trail off, into the debris and confusion in the wake of the Mississippi flood. What I needed was an experienced reader. I found one in Lambert Davis, an editor at Harcourt Brace who had once seen some of my photographs and texts. After several weeks, and the opinion of a second reader, he said Harcourt Brace was interested in the novel but felt that it needed a new conclusion. I agreed. It occurred to me, on reflection, that the experience I had had in Greenville, and had attempted to recapture in Santa Fe, might well serve as the basis for a conclusion to *My Uncle Dudley*. On days when I needed a rest from the darkroom I applied myself to reworking the novel.

In the early fall of 1941, with a portfolio of photographs and texts, I appeared at the Guggenheim Foundation and met Henry Allen Moe. In my allotted time, perhaps fifteen minutes, I tried to compress the facts and the fiction of my commitment to photographs and words. A keen and sympathetic listener, a matchless chain smoker, Mr. Moe gave me warm friendly glances through the veil of smoke between us. Did he feel I might try for a fellowship? He thought I might. I went away in a fever that found some release in the lyrical statement that went along with my application. I have been spared reexposure to my enthusiasm, but I suspect it embraced a passionate desire to salvage the barns, houses and structures of America before they dissolved into thin air. I had no idea, at the time I wrote it, how quickly it would happen.

Shortly after Pearl Harbor I learned of my father's death in Chicago. He had not written to me, nor I to him, for several years. When I left for college in California, in

1930, we had gone our separate ways. This story of a father and son who share a varied and adventurous life without the benefits or hazards of communication was more commonplace than unusual, one of the staple ingredients of the American novel and the emerging problems of alienation. This story is told in *Will's Boy*, published in 1981. The impact of my father's death would not assert itself until several years later, when I began to write the story of Will Brady, in *The Works of Love*. The emotions we had seldom shared as father and son preoccupied me to the exclusion of everything else, but I sensed none of this in the dark winter of 1941-42. I served as the building's air raid warden, and spent many evenings on the roof watching the lights of Manhattan blink off during the blackouts. The few that persisted glowed like planets.

I often sat there with my friend Sigmund Bekersky, a giant from the Ukraine who made his living as a nightclub bouncer. Bekersky had the talent to share the lives of many people with a few words of greeting and affection. He would come to the apartment with two quarts of milk, a loaf of whole wheat bread and a piece of smoked pork butt he would eat like a hotdog. Sprawled on a chair, his shirt unbuttoned, the two kittens would tunnel and crawl about his huge torso, licking greedily at his armpits. How he would roar! An ad in the Times lured him to Ohio where a handyman was wanted to help with chicken farming. In this way the wily Odysseus adapted to modern times.

In March I learned I had received a Guggenheim Fellowship. This news marked the summit of the great expectations I had been possessed by for several years. The long apprenticeship I had spent as a writer, and the increasing enthusiasm I felt for the prospect of joining photographs and words, prepared me for the elation I felt in this recognition. Like others before me, I pondered how to live to the fullest extent on this huge bounty, a sum of $2,500. Having lived well for years on less than half of that sum in California, that was where we headed.

On our previous trip west, if we were crossing Nebraska, I would drive most of the night while my wife slept in the seat. On this trip I felt the stirrings, however reluctant, of my plains boyhood. My father's death had awakened in me an interest in the past. In Omaha we drove past the places I had lived in as a boy. The houses seemed smaller, the hills and streets less steep, as if they had shrunken in my absence.

From Omaha we drove northwest toward Uncle Harry's farm, near Norfolk, where as a boy I had once spent two weeks of a summer vacation. On the dirt road south of town I stopped a passing car to ask if they knew of Harry Morris' farm.

"Do I *know* of him?" he replied. I nodded. He turned to spit into the ditch grass before replying. "Where you people from?" he said, unable to see the car license. I said that I was originally from Central City. "I didn't think you was from around here," he said, and let out the clutch.

I found my uncle's farm where he said it would be, but from the graveled road it looked abandoned. The porch and stoop were lacking from the front of the house, but I recalled that it had never had either. The only door to the house that was used was at the rear. I drove down the shrub-lined driveway to the back and parked the car in the chicken-scratched mounds near the barn. The long yard between the house and the barn, once green as a billiard table, was a thicket of matted grass and half buried croquet wickets. Doors tilted in shed doorways, fences were down, the dead trees of an orchard stood in weeds near the house, every visible object, wagon, implement and structure seemed to be at the end of a losing battle. The peeled branches of long dead trees arched over the house. Never before had I set eyes on such a mockery of my remembrance. If my wife had not been with me, I might have sneaked off. A few mangy bare-bottomed old hens clucked nervously as I walked toward the porch. The screen door, although poked full of holes, was latched. A water pail, floating the handle of the dipper, sat on the table to the left of the door. A draft smelling of pickling beets assailed me from the kitchen. Flies buzzed on both sides of the rusty screen. I called out, but nobody answered. I called again and heard one of the plates shift on the kitchen range. In a moment she appeared, a woman thin as a lath, a faded frock hanging limp from her shoulders. Over the frock a beet-stained apron, the ties dangling. Over her left eye she placed the fingers of one hand. The other stared at me unblinking. It seemed she did not recognize me, but I knew her.

"You don't remember me?" I asked. She didn't seem to. "I'm Will's boy, Wright," I said. It took a moment's time and effort to place me. Her tongue passed slowly over her store teeth.

"You've grown," she said flatly, and unlatched the screen. As she shooed out the flies she noted the car, and its passenger, parked near the barn. "Why don't you folks come in out of the heat?" she said, and waited until I had gone back and fetched my wife. "How's your father?" she said, when I entered the house, but she did not wait for my answer. She had never liked the man who had once sent her three crates of cholera-exposed Leghorn pullets. She had never liked Leghorns. Her idea of a laying and stewing chicken was the Plymouth Rock.

I can no longer distinguish between that actual meeting with Clara, in June, and the fiction I wrote about it that winter in California, the sentiments and nostalgia as palpable as the smell of pickling beets in the kitchen. I know we sat in the parlor, facing Clara in her rocker, and that the two women talked. Only her fan stirred the air in the room. It was of interest to her that I was married, and she inquired about my wife's people. Ohio she knew, having crossed it on her way west from Massachusetts. In the glare of light from the newly graveled road her face gleamed with perspiration. The rocker creaked. I noted the holes it had worn in the Axminster rug.

Some moments before he appeared, my Uncle Harry stopped on the back porch to skim flies off the bucket of water and toss them through the screen. Clara identified who we were, and reminded him that I had once spent some time on the farm. His watery blue eyes gave no sign of recognition. That I was seated in his chair confronted him with a problem only resolved when I surrendered it to him. He silently gazed at the light glare over the fields. We sipped warm water from the amber glasses that were usually stored on the top shelf in the cupboard.

This brief afternoon, during which I said little, listening to the voices of the women, would leave on me an impression from which I would never fully recover, repeatedly returning to the images, and the beet-pickled emotions, of that sultry summer day. In the car was my camera, but I could no more take photographs of what I saw around me than arrange for snapshots of the Second Coming. Images and emotions had saturated my limited responses. I was drugged by feelings that both moved and disturbed me. Had my father's death left in me a core of sorrow that would be responsive to these revisitations?

We drove south from Norfolk to my hometown of Central City, becalmed in the heat and the continuing Depression. Idle farmers sat in the gloom of a tin roofed pool hall. 5¢ cigars were selling for 4¢. I seemed unaware of ties or attachments. Down the road ten miles was Chapman, where my mother was buried, and I stopped at the barber shop to inquire if anyone might have known my mother or father. My father had once been an agent in Chapman, for the railroad, and my mother had been born on the bluffs just south of the river. As I entered his shop the barber studied my face in his wall mirror. "Don't you tell me," he said, "I'll tell you. You're Will and Grace's boy, aren't you?" I said I was. To my knowledge he had never before set eyes on me. His name was Eddie Cahow. At the turn of the century he had come up from Texas on the Chisholm Trail, but found he liked barbering better than trail riding. In the shop, waiting his turn at the chair, was Mr. Applegate, a farmer who had once courted one of my mother's sisters. For more than forty years he had kept the house she lived in in good repair.

Eddie Cahow was agreeable to my taking pictures inside his shop. I worked fast, fearing that so much of my visible past might disappear before I had caught it. Everything in the shop proved to be of interest. The mirror, with its chalked menu of services and prices, the tonic bottles and brushes on the chiffonier (PLATE 35), the case of razors and towels, the postcards sent to Cahow from traveling natives, tucked into the mirror's rim, the barber chair (PLATE 34), the sink with its platter for hair massages, the peanut machine, the benches with the plywood seats, the wall of calendar pictures of prize beef and kittens (PLATE 36). At the back of the shop, shipped out from Kansas City, was an elegant oak and iron grill that served as a bank, with its teller's window, the top ornamented with cans of flowering plants with trailing vines and tendrils (PLATE 37). I took several packs of film, the light being good from the large half-curtained window. Later we followed Mr. Applegate to the top of the bluffs where we saw the house my mother had been born and raised in, with its cupola affording a view of the river valley. Mr. Applegate's sisters, who had kept house for him since he had been spurned by one of my mother's sisters, brought a shoebox out of hiding to show me photographs of my mother's family. The sentiments this one day aroused are still fresh in my mind.

This meeting with Eddie Cahow, his barber shop, and his friends, would lock me into a pact with the bygone that I had begun on the farm near Norfolk. By the time we left, early in the evening, the setting sun burning on the windshield, I was committed to the recovery of a past I had only dimly sensed that I possessed. I was blissfully ignorant of any awareness that this would prove to be the work of a lifetime.

Time has an elusive shimmer in Southern California, both dazzling and insubstantial. One day follows another, one tremor follows another, it is hot in the sun but cool in the shadows, dark in the movie palace, dim in the rooms where the shades are lowered, a basking void of sunning, shopping, waiting, agreeable to those with a life to remember, but disquieting to those with a life to be lived. I spent my time working on the text for *The Inhabitants* and a novel, *The Man Who Was There*, that grew out of my impressions of the home place and Eddie Cahow's barbershop.

In the summer of 1944 we headed east, for Bryn Mawr, where my wife would teach at the Baldwin School for Girls. Along the way, in the high country of Colorado, we came on the general store in Kokomo—like the house in Culpeper—sitting for its portrait (PLATE 52). More pictures were taken in Silver Plume, a mining ghost town, the silence filled with the murmuring purl of water music visible through the cracks in the wooden sidewalk.

Crossing the plains to the east it's all down hill. As the long and empty freight trains clattered by us, with their litany of towns, states and places, the Baltimore and Ohio, the Burlington and Quincy, the Atchison, Topeka & Santa Fe, I began to dream of a series of books that would deal with the migration of Americans, a subject I knew something about. From the farm to the village, the village to the town, the town to the city, the city to the BIG town, and then once more—as I had lived it—back to the open road, irresistibly drawn westward. The farm at Norfolk would be the point of origin, then a small town like Central City, or Chapman, with a barber like Eddie Cahow, then a bigger town, then perhaps New York, and then—but much of that would wait on living, rather than planning. With such landscape in mind I did not feel pressed to make *The Inhabitants* a more inclusive volume, greatly increasing its size, and its production costs. With each mile we moved eastward I recovered the excitement that the stay in California had put on the back burner. Time had slowed, with the absence of the seasons and the light glare at the windows, but once we had crossed the Missouri I could once again hear its pulsing, driving, life-enhancing tick. Just twenty years before my father had also heard it, crossing from Omaha to Council Bluffs, where it had ticked off for him a passage that was inescapably downward. In the nature of things—as the scenario would have it—the son should share this passage with his father. And soon enough, in the writing of *The Works of Love*, he did.

The persuasion my wife exerted on influential administrators, educators and real estate agents made it possible for us to acquire an attractive apartment not far from the school. This was at the beginning of the housing shortage, and the dwelling had been altered to accommodate two families. A few weeks after we had settled in we had upstairs neighbors who proved to be from Nebraska. Loren Eiseley and his wife Mabel had come from Oberlin to spend a year as visiting professor at the University of Pennsylvania. We proved to have much in common. Eiseley was a poet, an aspiring writer and a distinguished anthropologist, and we shared similar dim views of the world. This was the start of a friendship during which we saw each other on a weekly basis. We had in common our plains background, which flowed underground, like

Platte River water, and our love of books. Book hunting and buying joined our two families in a common burden. We needed, and found in each other, support for our private demons.

There was no space in the house for a darkroom, so I turned my attention to writing. On one of my visits to New York I met Maxwell Perkins, of Charles Scribner's Sons. He turned his profile to me, his hearing aid, and occasionally he beamed on me his shy avuncular smile. I liked him immensely. I also sensed that my disorderly novel, *The Man Who Was There*, both pleased and distressed him. He liked novels that were longer, and less experimental. Still palpable to me, in his curtained office, were some of novelist Thomas Wolfe's great and endless expectations. I felt them as a burden. How did one fill such enormous shoes?

A year or more later I appeared in his office with my portfolio of photographs and texts, *The Inhabitants*. He seemed interested, but the format was unwieldy, the relationship between the words and images obscure. I peered around at the walls of his curtained office. High windows gave a view of the Child's restaurant on Fifth Avenue. With his permission, I took a handful of paper clips from his desk and began to clip the mounted photographs with the texts to the office curtains. The stratagem seemed to work. He watched me with an indulgent, bemused smile. I managed to put up more than half the volume, and I promised to take them down on my next visit. Two weeks passed before I returned, but the photographs and texts were where I had left them.

What did he think? He tilted back in his chair, thumbs hooked in his vest, the wide brimmed hat pushed back on his head. A familiar and often remarked posture. The smile he gave me needed no elaboration. He said he had no choice, regrettably, but to publish *The Inhabitants*. It would be done inexpensively, so that the host of readers he anticipated could afford the book. I feel that one of the book's signal triumphs was the impression it made on Max Perkins, and his decision that it should be published by Scribner's. There was no precedent for such an undertaking there, and this may have worked to the book's advantage in that I had a voice in all of the production decisions. I wanted the photographs to "bleed" rather than be enclosed by the page. A suitable paper was lacking at the time, but several coats of varnish gave the pages the appearance of glossy prints. The large format of the book pleased me immensely, and I am still staggered to read on the jacket that it sold for $3.75! At such a price Perkins was confident it would sell.

The Inhabitants was "well received," with excellent reviews, but the public did not buy it and the booksellers had no place to *put* it. Only the art book table would

Two-page spread from The Inhabitants, *1946*

accommodate the large format. A year later, in a shop on 23rd Street, I bought remaindered copies for 79¢, and *Let Us Now Praise Famous Men* for 39¢. I still have the last of ten copies I bought at that time.

In 1946 I applied for a second Guggenheim Fellowship, and I was fortunate enough to receive it. I exchanged my 3¼ x 4¼ view camera for a 4 x 5. In early May of the following spring I drove back to the farm near Norfolk. The Depression ravaged dirt farm of my previous visit was partially concealed and softened by the growth of spring, weeds concealed implements, a gone-to-seed over-ripeness seemed appropriate. I found my Uncle Harry at his ease, smoking a cob pipe, tinkering with an inner tube. Clara was more resigned than bitter. I found her seated in her rocker, her lap full of eggs, chipping at the dung spots with her thumb nail. To my suggestion that I would like to take pictures they expressed no objection. Did they know what I had in mind?

They had seen *The Inhabitants*. Feeling the need to justify, rather than explain, I said I wanted to capture what it was like to have lived on a dirt farm for half a century. There was no comment. I recall Clara moving her head from one side to the other, to see the room she sat in. Her shoes were unlaced. The ties of her apron dangled on the floor. I could hear mice stirring in the kitchen's basket of cobs. "I don't know why," she said, "but if it's what you want to do, you're free to."

It had never crossed my mind that she would give me leave to the *inside* of her house. I was about to reassure her, *You can trust me Clara*—trust me to do what? Wasn't I too greedy to be trusted? Didn't I privately feel I had earned this access? Just a few weeks before I had come on a statement, by Henry James in *The American Scene*, that gave me, I felt, unlimited access.

. . . is to be subject to the superstition that objects and places, coherently grouped, disposed for human use and addressed to it, must have a sense of their own, a mystic meaning proper to themselves to give out: to give out, that is, to the participant at once so interested and so detached as to be moved to a report of the matter.

I was hardly detached, but otherwise I was qualified. These objects and places spoke to me profoundly, and I was moved to a report of the matter. My Uncle Harry was indifferent to the nuances of exposure. The young man with his camera had come at a time when the usual reservations were in abeyance. For Clara, the whole farm was a ruin, an accumulation of losses, a disaster that her protestant soul must accept, and here comes this youth, a prodigal relation, who saw in these sorry remains something of value. She could not imagine what, but she could believe it was what he saw. The reservations of a lifetime would struggle in her soul with the dim, unlikely hope that the youth might be right.

At the end of the first day, one of a steady drizzle, I had brought my camera on its tripod in from the porch to make sure it was out of the rain. I stood it up in a dark corner of the kitchen, the lens reflecting the lampglow. Clara gazed at it for a moment with her good eye.

"It's not taking pictures now?" she asked me. I assured her it wasn't. "Just so I'm not in them," she said, and glanced down her flat, faded frock. Would anything convince her there was something of value in what she saw?

I was put in the upstairs bedroom I had had as a boy, almost thirty years before. The window frame was just a few inches off the floor, due to some miscalculation, the folds of the gathered lace curtain as dry and crisp as paper. The storm window, put up several years before, had not been taken down. On the doily of the bureau a satin lined box that had once contained an ivory handled comb, mirror and brush set, now held several corroded rifle cartridges and the partial handle of the missing mirror. Why had she preserved it? We were alike in that we perceived these objects in the light of our emotions and judged this the mystic meaning they had to give out.

At the start my Uncle Harry ignored me. I saw him pass with a hoe, with a pail of water, with another inner tube that needed repairing, indifferent to my presence. I drew him in with questions. Would it rain again? He replied that it usually did. Soon he trailed me around, offered dry suggestions, tested me with his dead pan humor. He still smoked Union Leader, if and when he could find his pipe. When I suggested a picture of himself—the greatest ruin of all—he was compliant. Actually, he had been waiting. In the museum of relics the farm had become he was one of the few that still almost worked. He pointed that out himself.

I had him walk before me, through the door of the barn he had entered and exited for half a century (PLATE 1). He had become, like the denims he wore, an implement of labor, one of the discarded farm tools. A personal pride, however, dormant since the Depression, reasserted itself in the way he accepted my appreciative comments. Why not? Had he not endured and survived it all, like the farm itself? Over several days I had remarked that he changed his hats according to the time of day and the occasion. A sporty nautical number in the early morning, at high noon and afternoon one of his wide brimmed straws. In the dusk of evening he preferred an old felt, with a narrow brim, the color and texture of tar paper. All hats suited him fine. The only piece of apparel we both found out of fashion was new overalls, blue stripes on white, that in no way adapted to his figure or movements and gave off the rasp of a file. He was quick to sense my disapproval and stopped wearing them.

It was Clara's suggestion that I might look in on Ed's place. Ed was a bachelor, related by marriage, who had died several weeks before my arrival. His small farmhouse was directly across the road. The bed had been made, but otherwise I found the house as a bachelor would have left it. The bric brack of a lifetime, pill boxes, pin cushions, shotgun shells, flashlights, a watch and chain, a few snapshots. Although the bed had been made, the imprint of his body remained, his feet were almost visible in the shoes beneath it. What I saw on the ground glass evoked in me a commingling of tenderness, pity and sorrow, to the exclusion of more searing emotions. Was there another American emotion to match it? Were not tragic sentiments

alien to a free people who were free to choose, and chose more earthly adornments? "Ed passed on last month," Harry had said, as if he had glanced just a bit too late to catch him. What he seemed to see was a movement of the bushes edging the drive.

One evening Clara had shown me a photograph of the Morris family, taken in Ohio in the late 1880s, showing all members of the family, except my father and Harry, forming a line in front of a clapboard house in a fresh fall of snow. Their names had been read aloud to me by Harry—Mitchell and Emerson, Ivy and Mae, Martha and Francena—on and on through a dozen. A crack in time had been made by the click of a shutter, through which I could peer into a world that had vanished. This fact exceeded my grasp, but it excited my emotions. The following day I took the photograph into the open air and pinned it to the clapboards on one side of the house. I saw it clearly on the ground glass before the shutter clicked. Was it in this way I hoped to postpone what was vanishing? A simpler ritual of survival would be hard to imagine. By stopping time I hoped to suspend mortality.

Since I had taken all of the interior shots without artificial lighting I was anxious to get the negatives developed and see what I had done. In Lincoln, while they were being processed, I drove around through the neighboring towns and found many structures of interest. A weathered church near Milford (PLATE 27), a railroad station in Panama, a barber pole and barber shop in Weeping Water (PLATE 38), in which the photographer can be seen in the mirror. In Central City I woke up the barber, dozing in his chair after lunch. He remembered my father—a railroad man who had turned to raising chickens—but he had no memory of the boy who had sat on the board placed on the chair arms, heard the chirp of the shears and smelled the tonic water doused on his hair. There had been a lot of boys. Looking at me, front and side, brought none of them to mind.

With the negatives in hand I was eager to get back to work in the darkroom. During the three days of driving east I pondered what I should have as a text. Why not such an experience as I had just had, the return of a long prodigal native? Better yet, let him return with his family, a big city girl and two city kids who had never corked the holes in a privy. Let them all respond to the objects and places for which they had few, if any, mystic feelings. The smell of pickling beets, the heat from a cob burning range, the flies to be skimmed off the bucket of water, would have on a city girl an effect more in the line of nausea than nostalgia. More in the line of what this homecoming would need. What would bring them back to such a farm in the first place? The housing shortage in the cities. The need for a place to live. I was so well primed with this story, and it so well suited my emotions, that I postponed the darkroom work and spent the first several weeks writing. Especially fragrant to me was the remembered smell of the beets.

The Home Place, published in 1948, proved to be a radical departure from *The Inhabitants*. The text would be a narration of one day's events, as told by the returning native, and each page of text would face a photograph. The relationship would sometimes be explicit—the object photographed would be mentioned—but in the main the photographs would provide the visible ambience for the story, as if we walked about the farm while listening to the narration. The format would be much smaller than *The Inhabitants*, roughly the size of a novel, and the photographs would be cropped. These mutilations removed them, as a group, from the context of artworks, as "images," and presented them as "things" and artifacts. The decision to do the book

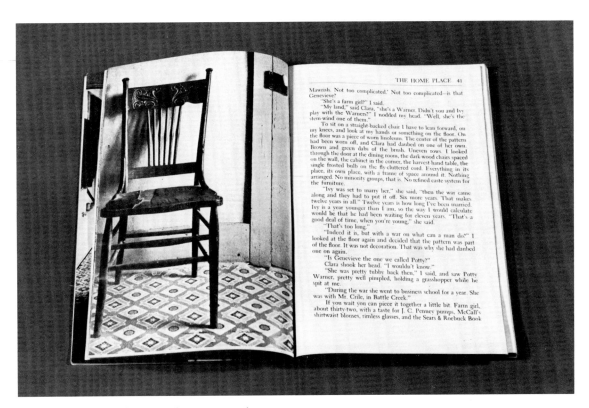

Two-page spread from The Home Place, *1948*

in this manner permitted no compromise. I wanted to know what such a book would be like, and I found out. The readers I had in mind—it was part of my euphoria—were those who would browse through the book like an album. Most of the readers I found objected to the distraction of the photographs, and those who liked the photographs largely ignored the text. The book was very well received, critically, and continues to find reader-lookers, but it was not bought at the time of publication and confused many reviewers about the author. Was he a writer, who took photographs, or a photographer who did a little writing? The public is ill at ease with the ambidextrous. The writer who does a little painting on the side is not felt to be a "committed" writer. Or painter. My publisher read these reviews, checked the sales figures, and suggested, sensibly, that I stick to my "proper business" as a novelist. I was angered, injured, hit between wind and high water, grievously disappointed—but I listened. Photo-text books were expensive to produce, and on both books Scribner's had lost money. In the volume on which I was then at work, *The World in the Attic*, the second in the series of photo-text books I had planned, I was persuaded to give up the photographs. This book continued the story of the Muncy family, after they leave the home place, and provides Clyde Muncy, and the author, with deep mind-clearing draughts of small

49

town nausea. This I very much needed, after *The Home Place*, but more important, in the character of Tom Scanlon, I acquired a key to my future as a novelist, a freshet of emotion, memory and imagination that would prove to be inexhaustible.

At a gathering of photographers—perhaps one of the first—sponsored by Edward Steichen at The Museum of Modern Art, I met Walker Evans, Ben Shahn, Charles Sheeler and numerous others who were full of plans, talk and stimulating controversy. Some of us walked the streets and talked until far into the morning. *The Home Place* had just been published, to high praise from Lewis Mumford, but "straight" photographers were not lacking who saw photo-text as a dangerous corruption. It seemed and was, however, a very good and productive time for the making of photographs, books and talk.

In the early fifties I continued to take photographs and made several trips back to the Midwest, as far as Nebraska. Some photo-text essays appeared in *The New York Times Magazine* during this period but I became increasingly preoccupied with my writing.

In Los Angeles, in the spring of 1958, I met a young woman, Josephine Kantor, an art collector and dealer who was interested in contemporary painting, and in a few days time, before she left for Paris, I tried to persuade her to be interested in me. Jo Kantor knew many of the painters of the period, Motherwell, Rothko and Diebenkorn among them, and was influential in promoting their work in California. That fall we met in Paris and later that winter in Mexico City. In the spring of 1959 we sailed from New York to Venice for our first long stay of seven months. On returning to California I obtained a divorce from my first wife and Jo and I were married. We lived briefly in Pacific Palisades, spent another spring and summer in Venice, then returned to California, in the fall of 1962. We settled in Mill Valley, across the Gate from San Francisco, where I joined the faculty of San Francisco State University to teach literature and creative writing, until 1975.

A visit from John Szarkowski, in the mid-sixties, reminded me that I was a photographer. I had no new photographs, but as I browsed through the old ones I noted the change in my response to the same images. They were the same, but I had altered. I was ripe with the memories and emotions that had not previously found expression. The result of this was *God's Country and My People*, a very personal revisitation to both a real and an imaginary landscape, one I had been for many years creating as a writer. This recombining of the visual and the verbal, full of my own kind of unpeopled portraits, sought to salvage what I considered threatened, and to hold fast to what was vanishing. Samuel Beckett had put it memorably:

Let me try and explain. From things about to disappear I turn away in time. To watch them out of sight, no, I can't do it.

In April of 1969 Jo and I returned to Venice, which we had last visited in 1962. On the two previous occasions we had settled in Venice, for periods of six and seven months, I had gone to work. That very dry place novel, *Ceremony in Lone Tree*, was completed during a lovely and relatively humid Venetian summer. On this visit we planned to enjoy the city in the manner for which it was conceived. We strolled around, loitered, rode the *vaporettos* and sat under the umbrellas sipping espressos. We were at home in Venice, in the manner of exiles, and had once laid plans to live there. Not knowing when, if ever, we might return, I brought along a mini camera, a Rollei 35, and took Kodachrome slides as we wandered about the city. I had these rolls developed, as they were taken, and we liked what we saw in the slide viewer.

On our return to California, Peter Mollman, of Harper & Row, a Venice enthusiast, paid us a visit. I showed him the slides I had taken, and he suggested that we should have a book. That would require something special in the way of a text, and I was not free at the time to work on it. A year later, while I was teaching at Princeton, I wrote the text for *Love Affair: A Venetian Journal*, a narration that reflected our own experience. Like so many of the objects and places in my life, Venice too was threatened by air pollution, high tides and crumbling foundations. It had recently been suggested that an elevated motor ramp, circling the city, would provide tourists with a more intimate view without the unthinkable thought of actual motor traffic. Sentiments anticipating the demise of Venice have surely enhanced her charms for centuries. My text had in mind the quotidian side of what it was like to live in Venice, possessed by an unflagging enchantment. Only the mid-summer *sirocco*, the becalmed torpor of humidity, heat and canal exhalations, seriously threatened our attachment. We were then, and remain, hooked.

The color plates for *Love Affair* were made by the Amilcare Pizzi press, of Milan, and at one point in the production one of the slides was lost. For weeks it was searched for, in vain. The loss of the slide meant that the final correction of the plate could not be made. The plate in question was of a structure in what had once been the Jewish ghetto. The muted, uncorrected color of this plate, when I finally saw it, seemed appropriate to the subject. Months after the book was published the missing slide was found where most missing slides go, and should first be looked for—in the trap beneath the slide projector.

Appropriate to this occasion is the postword. A member of the Pizzi firm, who had lived in Venice, had returned to the city with a camera to take the same picture from the exact same spot. He found the spot, but it proved to be one of the few structures that had been repainted.

During our stay at Princeton Peter Bunnell offered me the use of the art department darkroom, and I used the occasion to make the first prints in almost twenty years. This aroused the long dormant photographer in me, but on reflection both Jo and I felt it would prove to be a distraction I should avoid, since once we were back in California I would not have access to a darkroom.

Three years later, in the fall of 1975, the University of Nebraska, in Lincoln, planned a series of lectures on my work. As part of this occasion Norman Geske, director of the Sheldon Memorial Art Gallery on the campus, scheduled a retrospective exhibition of my photographs. Jim Alinder, who was then the director of the photography program in the University's Art Department, made the necessary prints from a selection of my negatives. Jim's darkroom expertise, along with his familiarity with and affection for my work, resulted in prints that were frequently superior to those I had managed to make in the past. This show of 200 prints was hung in October, and Jim supervised the production of a handsome catalogue, *Structures and Artifacts*, in which 100 of the prints were reproduced. Over the next four years the show was exhibited in museums about the country.

In 1979 Neil Rappaport, of the photography department of Bennington College, asked me to come to Bennington and talk to his students. For a six week period, during May and June, we enjoyed a matchless Vermont spring while I talked about photography.

On our way home from Vermont, on a stop in New York, Jo and I had a visit with our friend Eugene Prakapas, who had exhibited my photographs in the late seventies, and we made the acquaintance of Lee Witkin in his gallery on 57th Street. Lee proved to be a collector and reader of my novels, as well as of my photo-text books, and on his next trip to California he came to see us in Mill Valley. On a subsequent visit he brought up the possibility of a Witkin-Berley portfolio. The physical work involved was formidable. The first and greatest obstacle was that I had no darkroom, and photographers are reluctant to share them. The sensible thing to have done, of course, was to have said no—so we said yes. I say we because without Jo's support and assistance the enterprise would have been impossible. On the positive side, I was actually eager to reexperience the unrivaled seance of the darkroom which, with the assistance of friends, we installed in our home in July. By late fall the work was done. In January 1981 the portfolio was completed and exhibited at the Witkin Gallery.

Almost half a century after I first attempted to link my eye to that of the camera, in Vienna, I spoke to the Society for Photographic Education at Asilomar, in Pacific Grove, California, on *The Camera Eye*. In recent years I've had reason to ponder, as Niepce did in 1832, the enigmatic nature of the photographic image. It is at once immediate, available and elusive. Andre Bazin's comment seems to me the most perceptive and provocative.

All the arts are based on the presence of man, but only photography gains an advantage from his absence.

My own reflections can be found in "In Our Image" (*The Massachusetts Review*), "Photographs, Images and Words" (*The American Scholar*), and "The Camera Eye" (*Exposure*).

Although we might describe this as the photographic century, the nature and singularity of the photographic image still eludes us. In the face of all evidence to the contrary, we persist in feeling, if not in believing, that facts are what photographs give us, and that however much they lie, they do so with the raw materials of truth.

The simplest snapshot, in its seamless commingling of time's presence and its suspension, testifies to the photograph's ineluctable nature. At once commonplace and unearthly, it arouses us in a way that exceeds our comprehension, yet involves us in time's ineffable mystery. For a bewildering moment we are free of our time-bound selves.

The dawn of consciousness may be the dawn of time as perceived by man. From that first moment of awareness man has sought a piece of time's living substance, an arrested moment that would authenticate time's existence. Not the ruin of time, nor the tombs of time, but the eternal present in time's every moment. From this spinning reel of time the camera snips a sampling of the living tissue, along with the distortions, the illusions and the lies, a specimen of the truth.

Where time is captured in repose, and is seemingly timeless, its fleeting presence is visible in the ghostly blur of a passing figure, the actual track of time's passage. The carriage crossing a square, the pet straining at its leash, are momentarily detained from their destination. On these ghostly shades the photograph confers a brief immortality.

In its unexampled directness the photograph has enjoyed, until recently, an unrivaled artlessness of communication. But now that it has undergone a rise in status, and is an object of value and speculation, the attention it receives is increasingly verbal. Words now affirm the photographic image, as photographs once confirmed reality. This seems to be the fate of all enterprises that are open to scrutiny and discussion. To the extent the photograph is a ponderable object, it will have to be pondered with words.

Would this be one reason why words are so notably lacking from Walker Evans' volume, *First and Last*, where a few would be helpful, and photographs are absent from Susan Sontag's book *On Photography*? This bizarre polarity comprehends the photographic scene, where picture-making is giving way to analysis and stock-taking. Feverishly self-aware, and as ambitious as life, photography now ponders its many selves. Rather than another likeness, the photo image has become a thing in itself.

Nevertheless, it is appropriate that these new images take their place among the objects we value. They reveal our shared awareness of the world around us, and lift the veil on the mysterious world within us. Photographs now confirm all that is visible, and photographs will affirm what is one day remembered. Many images compete for the 20th century, and the camera eye has been a steady and impartial witness, but I would guess that planet earth, seen rising on the moon's horizon, will vibrate the longest in human memory. While we continue to grope, like Niepce, for the precise words to capture what the photograph is, the highest praise should be reserved for what continues to elude us. The photographic dilemma, to the extent that there is one, lies with the photographer, not the photograph.

However varying their points of view, all photographers share the common field of vision that the mind's eye, and the camera's eye, has imposed on this century. Quite beyond the telling of it, as well as the seeing of it, exceeding both our criticism and our appreciation, the camera's eye combines how we see with whatever is there to be seen. What it has in mind for us may not at all be what we have in mind for ourselves.

Photographs

PLATE I   Uncle Harry, Home Place, Norfolk, Nebraska, 1947

PLATE 2   Clothes on Hooks, Home Place, 1947

PLATE 3   Eggs in Pot, Home Place, 1947

PLATE 4   Reflection in Oval Mirror, Home Place, 1947

PLATE 5   Stove and View of Parlor, Home Place, 1947

PLATE 6   Through the Lace Curtain, Home Place, 1947

PLATE 7 Screened Window with Curtains, Home Place, 1947

PLATE 8   Front Door, Home Place, 1947

PLATE 9   Rocker, Home Place, 1947

PLATE 10   Ed's Place, near Norfolk, Nebraska, 1947

PLATE II   Dresser Drawer, Ed's Place, 1947

PLATE 12   Kitchen Range, Ed's Place, 1947

PLATE 13   Living Room, Ed's Place, 1947

PLATE 14   Straightback Chair, Home Place, 1947

PLATE 15   Drawer with Silverware, Home Place, 1947

PLATE 16   Upstairs Bedroom, Home Place, 1947

PLATE 17   Bedroom, Home Place, 1947

PLATE 18   Bedroom with Portrait, Home Place, 1947

PLATE 23   School Outhouse and Backstop, Nebraska, 1947

PLATE 24   Mailboxes, Western Nebraska, 1947

PLATE 25   Farmhouse near McCook, Nebraska, 1940

PLATE 26   Abandoned Farm, Western Nebraska, 1941

PLATE 27   Church near Milford, Nebraska, 1947

PLATE 28   Farmhouse with Snowbank, near Lincoln, Nebraska, 1947

PLATE 29   House in Winter, near Lincoln, 1941

PLATE 30 Gano Grain Elevator, Western Kansas, 1940

PLATE 31   Light Pole and Grain Elevator, Nebraska, 1947

PLATE 32   Store Fronts, Western Kansas, 1940

PLATE 33   Barber Pole and Hydrant, Needles, California, 1938

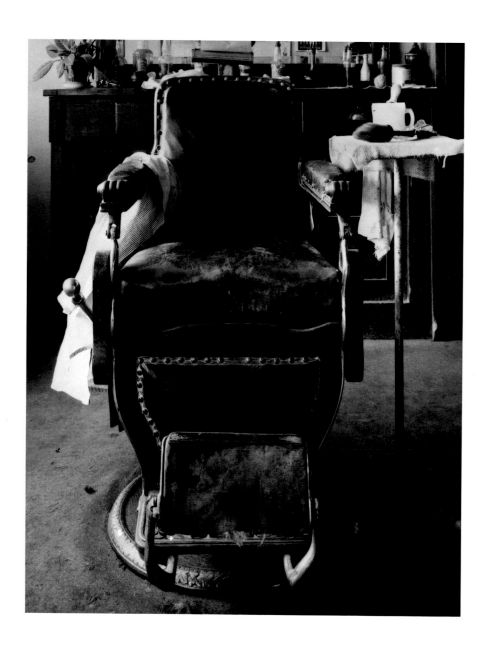

PLATE 34   Barber's Chair, Cahow's Barber Shop, Chapman, Nebraska, 1942

PLATE 35   Barber Shop Utensils and Cabinet, Cahow's Barber Shop, 1942

PLATE 36   Barber Shop Interior, Cahow's Barber Shop, 1942

PLATE 37   Bank Grill, Cahow's Barber Shop, 1942

PLATE 38   Barber Shop, Weeping Water, Nebraska, 1947

PLATE 39   Gumball Machine, Cahow's Barber Shop, 1942

PLATE 40   Visit the Lyric Tonite, Central City, Nebraska, 1947

PLATE 41   Haystack, near Norfolk, Nebraska, 1947

PLATE 42   Meeting House, Southbury, Connecticut, 1940

PLATE 43   Three Trees, Eastern Nebraska, 1947

PLATE 44   White House, Cape Cod, 1939

PLATE 45   White Church Facade, Rahway, New Jersey, 1940

PLATE 46   White Barn, Connecticut, 1940

PLATE 47   Rural Schoolhouse, Eastern Kansas, 1940

PLATE 48   Faulkner Country, near Oxford, Mississippi, 1940

PLATE 49   Power House and Palm Tree, near Lordsburg, New Mexico, 1940

PLATE 50   Adobe House with Wagon Wheel, New Mexico, 1940

PLATE 51 Adobe with Tire, New Mexico, 1940

PLATE 52   Kokomo, Colorado, 1944

PLATE 53   Tombstone, Arizona, 1940

PLATE 54   Houses on Incline, Virginia City, Nevada, 1941

PLATE 55   Church and House, Virginia City, 1941

PLATE 56   City Hall, Tecumseh, Nebraska, 1947

PLATE 57   Row House, Baltimore, 1940

PLATE 58   Bedroom and Washstand, Southern Indiana, 1950

PLATE 59   Dresser with Mirror, Southern Indiana, 1950

PLATE 60 Padded Rocker, Indiana, 1950

PLATE 61   Jukebox, Southern Indiana, 1950

ACKNOWLEDGEMENTS

The first hint of this book was in the photographic eye of Jim Alinder. The book's production is the fruitful collaborative effort of Jim and his colleagues, Peter A. Andersen and David Featherstone, all of whom challenged my preconceptions, corrected my lapses, and overwhelmed me with the results.

To my wife Jo Morris who contributed in the numberless ways to which I am so long accustomed.

David Gardner and his staff provided the matchless laser scan printing. To the many capable hands who must go unmentioned, my greetings and thanks.

Wright Morris

THE FRIENDS OF PHOTOGRAPHY

The Friends of Photography, founded in 1967, is a not-for-profit membership organization with headquarters in Carmel, California. The Friends actively supports and encourages creative photography through wide-ranging programs in publications, grants and awards to photographers, exhibitions, workshops, lectures and critical inquiry. The publications of The Friends, the primary benefit received by members of the organization, emphasize contemporary photography yet are also concerned with the criticism and history of the medium. They include a monthly newsletter, a quarterly journal and major photographic monographs. Membership is open to everyone. To receive an informational membership brochure write to the Membership Director, The Friends of Photography, Post Office Box 500, Carmel, California 93921.